This book makes the 943rd object I have dedicated to my fabulous wife, Kalin. That may seem excessive until one realizes that without her invaluable daily contribution to my life, my existence would mean less than that of a speck of bacteria under the hoof of a rotting yak in Tibet. At least, I *think* she said "under the hoof of a rotting yak in Tibet". But maybe she said "up on the roof with a plotting slack of barrettes". Either way, this book is dedicated to her.

I would also like to dedicate Stephen King's latest book to all my readers, friends and family. I don't know King personally, but I can't imagine that a guy who publishes seven major novels a month would mind if I borrowed one.

© Copyright 1989, 1990, 1991. All rights reserved. No part o' this book may be reproduced in any form without written permission from the publisher. Printed in the United States of A. Distributed in Canada by Raincoast Books, 112 East 3rd Ave. Vancouver, B.C. V5T 1C8
ISBN: 0-87701-854-5
10 9 8 7 6 5 4 3 2 1

Chronicle Books can be reached at: 275 Fifth St. San Francisco 94103
Not available in parts of Vanuatu.

33

40

41

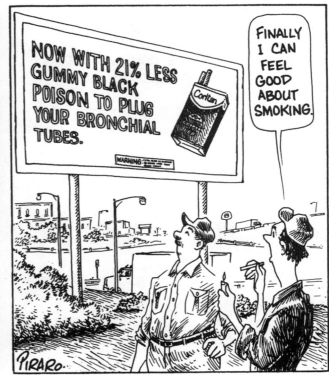

52

57

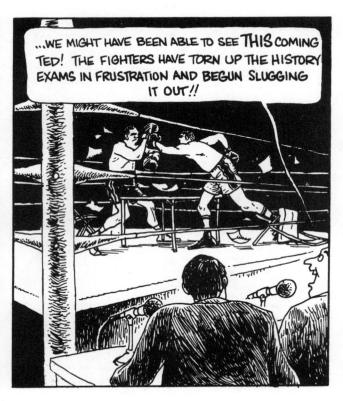

SUPERMAN'S OLDER BROTHER

EXECUTIVE MATERIAL

60

61

67

THE PACK OF GUM

73

RUNAWAY ESCALATOR

THE BENEFITS OF THE FAMILY HEALTH CLUB MEMBERSHIP.

80

AUDIENCE WITH THE LANDLORD

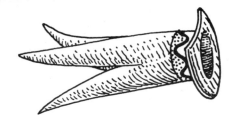

ABOUT THE AUTHOR

Dan Piraro stood nearly twice as tall as any household yardstick when he was killed in an upholstering accident six years ago. He was a loving father, a respected member of his community, and a stranger to no one who knew him well. Since that day, a steady stream of cartoons has been appearing in the file drawers of Chronicle Features, a newspaper syndication company in San Francisco known for keeping an ear to the spiritual world. Now in something less than a million newspapers worldwide, and in books published in five countries, Piraro enjoys continued success from beyond the grave. His royalty checks are left on a rocky hilltop in Montana where they disappear mysteriously after dark.